Five Steps
to
Being Heard

How to get your message across to the right person

Julie Cooper

ISBN 978-0-9559680-9-9

Published by Spring Publishing, an imprint of Careertrain Publishing

www.springpublishing.co.uk

hello@springpublishing.co.uk

Printed and bound in Great Britain

Note: The material contained in this book is set out in good faith for general guidance only and no liability can be accepted for loss or expense incurred as a result of relying in particular circumstances on statements made in this book.

Foreword

Being able to communicate and make an impact concerns a lot of people.

We know this because we've been sharing 360 degree feedback with clients for quite a while now, and we've seen it come up time and time again.

"Five Steps to Being Heard" takes all the building blocks of getting your message across, and puts them into a clearly defined structure that is easy to understand and remember.

It took me just an hour to read, and it was an hour well spent.

There may be some elements that you already know – it would be surprising if you didn't – but what you will learn is how to assemble them in a way that makes sense and gets results.

Getting your message across to the right person is critical; this enjoyable little book shows you how to do just that.

Happy reading.

Richard Oppenheimer

Richard is the founder and owner of Appraisal360 – provider of 360 degree feedback solutions. Learn more at **www.appraisal360.co.uk**

Contents

Why are you here?

This book is about how to make sure the relevant people in your life *really* hear you when you speak to them. You will stand a better chance of being influential, getting your point across and fulfilling your ambitions. After all, how can they give you the job you want, or the support, or the glory, if they don't know who you are, what you want and what you can do?

It's not about goal setting or helping you find direction. There are other resources and people that can help you with these. This book starts with some questions. If you struggle to come up with the answers, you might need to tackle these areas first, although you are likely to pick up some confidence building tips anyway.

You will have you own reasons for choosing to read this book. You probably have some idea what your motives are and what it is you would like to achieve.

Before we take the plunge and explain how to make sure you are noticed, I'd like you to spend a moment asking yourself exactly what it is you want from this book. I'm a big believer in clarifying our thoughts; Socrates was very wise when he said that understanding the question is half the answer. Take a couple of moments to bring sharp focus where you currently have woolly hopes. If you can't describe your thoughts accurately to yourself, you are not going to be able to convey them to anyone else, are you?

Here are some questions to help you explore and define your thoughts:

★ *What is it the world (or at least part of it) should know about you?*

Is it about your ability? If so, what exactly is it you can do well? How good are you? How do you know? Where is the proof? How are you different to other people who can do the same thing?

Is it about your values or ethics? Do you have strong beliefs that directly impact on how you operate and what you choose to do?

Is it about your personality? Do you want others to behave in a certain way around you? Do you have needs that are not being met? Do aspects of your personal style impact positively or negatively on those around you? Do you have traits or sensitivities that you would like others to take into account?

Is it about your ambition or direction? How you intend your life to be in the future? What you are aiming to achieve?

★ *Who should know?*

Your boss? Customers? Work colleagues? Potential employers? Key players in your network? Friends? Neighbours? Family? People you have yet to meet? The media?

★ *How would it benefit you if they did know?*

There has to be some advantage to make this worth your while. What would be different? Would you have better prospects? A more fulfilling career? Feel more satisfied because your talents are being used? Improved relationships?

The benefit might not be for you directly – think Bob Geldof and Band Aid (if you are old enough!). Sometimes we need to be noticed to change things for others. Is this about you, or a cause you care about?

The more specific and focused you are about what it is you want, the easier it is to be influential and articulate. Spend some time fine tuning your grand plan as much as you can. Add detail so that you can see the picture more clearly.

★ *...And if nothing changes?*

Will it really matter? Will you be upset, angry or disappointed? What are the long term implications? Or are you not really that bothered? Are you doing this because YOU want to, or someone tells you that you should? Or you think you 'ought'?

If you don't really mind if nothing changes, maybe you should examine your motivation and plans. If you're not committed and passionate, you are unlikely to convince others.

There are two more questions to answer before we start on the Five Steps:

- What is the message you want to get across?

- What are the reasons you are not being noticed as you want right now?

Let's explore these a little. Then we'll get down to business.

★ *What is the message you want to get across?*

Your answer may be a work in progress; this is fine. You can develop and refine it along the way as your thoughts become clearer. Get as much down on paper/screen as you can at *the* moment. Words, phrases, a mindmap, bubblegram or vision board are all useful tools to help you express yourself. Choose something that works for you, and be prepared to do a few drafts until you are happy with it.

If the message you want to convey varies for different audiences, you will need to do this exercise for every person you want to make a better connection with, An over arching *"This is my message"* statement can help to keep yourself on track.

Here is an example....

This is my message

I am a confident and competent administrator planning to develop my career into project management. I am capable of handling more responsibility and I'm actively looking for opportunities to do this to prove my worth. I meet deadlines, go the extra mile and deliver excellent value for money. I'm ready to step up.

Negatives not allowed. No way!

If you find yourself writing a string of negatives when you write your message down, there is something you need to do. Do you have negatives that look like any of these?

I'm not a dogsbody!

I should not be a coward. I need to stop letting everyone talk over me in meetings.

You never notice what I achieve.

I'm not stupid....

Get them all down, out of your head and on to paper or the screen - then take a deep breath and **turn them all round to positives.**

Why? Because of the way our brain works. Your brain won't notice the *'nots '*and *'can'ts '*– it will just register the adjectives, so swimming around inside your head will be *'Stupid, coward, dogsbody'...stupid, coward, dogsbody....'* Not quite the message you wanted to send, is it?

It's also not good for your mental well being if your key messages to yourself are negative – you are just wearing yourself down, and convincing yourself, slowly but surely, that you are stupid...Let's NOT go there!

Tell yourself here and now that you will begin to frame your thoughts positively. If you are not familiar with the concept of reframing, it wouldn't hurt to do a little research. It is a really useful habit to acquire, used by most highly successful people.

For example, if we turned those negative thoughts round they might look like this:

~~I'm not a dogsbody!~~

I am a valuable person with skills and potential.

~~I'm a coward I need to stop letting everyone talk over me in meetings.~~

I can speak up for myself.

I have ideas and thoughts to contribute.

* * *

~~You never notice what I achieve~~. I am proud of my achievements.

~~I'm not stupid....~~ I am capable and competent

Which gives us:

I am a valuable person with skills and potential.
I can speak up for myself.
I have ideas and thoughts to contribute.
I am proud of my achievements.
I am capable and competent.

Look at the difference between the negative and positive messages. What impression do they both give you? Which person would you rather be?

We are all works in progress. We need to be aware of the areas where we need to grow (we're just coming to that), but we also need to acknowledge our worth and the road we choose from here onwards. The only alternative is standing still and looking backwards. It's hard to move forward from there.

Lastly...

★ **What are the reasons you are not being noticed as you want right now?**

Although we don't want your key message to be negative, we don't live in Pollyanna Land where we blindly believe everything is perfect. It is important that we recognise our flaws, inconsistencies and weaknesses so that we can address them.

Be honest with yourself here. There are things holding you back, and you can't deal with them effectively if you don't know what they are. The same principle applies that we mentioned earlier - you need to know the question to find the answer.

This is a tough question to ask yourself. Below is a list of possible causes. Have a look through. Which ones apply to you? To what degree? Once you've mapped your issues, you can begin to tackle them.

- I lack confidence

- I am unsure what to say

- I fear embarrassment or ridicule

- My message is unclear

- I'm naturally quiet

- I don't know why anyone should listen to me.

- I don't get the opportunity to talk to the right audience

- I assume others know what I want and need, even if I haven't explicitly told them

- The time hasn't been right yet

- I am inconsistent. I change my mind about my needs.

- I send out mixed or conflicting messages

- My emotions get the better of me

- My reputation is tarnished by others

- I am talking to people who do not want to hear my message

- I'm careless about what I say in any company

- I spend too much time with people who drain or squash me

- I've grown out of my social circle but haven't moved on

- Some other reason?

It's a long list, isn't it? We are all unique, with a different set of drivers and personal traits, yet some of these them are common to many of us.

How to Overcome your Barriers

Spend a little time thinking about how you could overcome the key issues that are holding you back. Here are some pointers:

- Firstly, examine the issue. Where is the evidence? Is it really true, or is it a label that you've put on yourself, or someone else has attached to you? It may have been true once, that might not be the case now.

- Prioritise the issues, so that you can see what needs tackling first.

- Work at visualising what the preferred scenario looks like, so that you can work towards it.

- Generate a range of possible options for improving each one, then weigh up the options. Which gives the quickest win? Which takes the least resources? What is your gut telling you is the best way forward? Devise yourself an action plan, starting with the top priority (There is more about action planning later).

- Find a confidante to share your thoughts with. It could be a friend, a mentor, coach. It increases our action when we are accountable to another person.

The Five Steps will help you find insights to many of the barriers, by suggesting positive actions you can take.

Messages in Harmony

One important factor to mention here is congruence. This means having all parts of your message being consistent with each other.

If I told you I enjoyed public speaking, but was too shy to look you in the eye, what would you believe? If I told you I was a top-flight athlete, yet you could see I was overweight and wheezy, what would you think?

A spoken, face to face message has several parts. If the parts don't all agree with each other, alarm bells ring in the listener. They will dismiss or disbelieve you, making your job harder. You need to think about:

- How you sound −pitch, pace, tone.

- The words you choose

- Your visual impact – what you wear, grooming

- Your body language – poise, stance, gestures

You will have gathered from the examples above that the words you choose are not the most important part of your message. Body language will be believed over words every time, so make sure you pay attention to this, too.

Let's Go!

Enough navel gazing. You've thought through what you want to say and why you want to say it. You've got a plan for addressing your barriers. Let's get started.

Step One

★ Be interested

Imagine that you have written a beautiful handwritten letter sharing your deepest hopes and dreams. You put it in an envelope, add a stamp, and put it in the post box. There is no address on it. Where will it end up? There is no point in sending any message if you don't know where it's going. All your time and trouble in choosing your words and crafting the message will be wasted. This, in effect, is what you are doing if you try to get your point over, without knowing relevant information about the person you want to receive your message.

Why would you even try to deliver a message without knowing the recipient? Isn't this what we call junk mail or spam?

You might think you are not guilty, but do you know what, we all do it all the time. We think we know the other person yet we haven't taken the time to find out the facts we need to know how to pitch our message accurately.

What do we do instead? This is where it gets dangerous. We make assumptions, based possibly on our knowledge or observations, but often based on our perceptions, prejudices or opinion – and we often get it wrong. Result? We deliver the wrong message in the wrong way to a person who is not what we thought they were. Which is not a good result, is it?

Here's an example

Let's say you are getting flak at work because your company is late paying some of your suppliers. Every time you pick up the phone, it's someone complaining that their invoice is overdue. You decide to raise the matter with the company accountant. Yes, you know his role, and of course you are well within your rights to discuss work based issues with him, and he should act on your complaint.

But here's the 'but'… But what if there is a good reason, or other bigger issues going on? What if he has just had to fire his assistant for messing up the system? What if he has just had to take several weeks off because his child had a life threatening accident? What if there was a serious liquidity issue and the company literally did not have the money to make the payments on time?

The things going on in his life and work don't affect the facts about the late payments – but they could make a difference about how you to choose to approach him. You might select different words, or a different time – and it's very likely that your feelings about the situation will alter too.

You can only choose the most appropriate approach if you know the other person's circumstances.

Not only will finding out about people help you know how to target and pitch what you want to say, it can also open up new opportunities and avenues to explore. Who knew that the secretary's husband works in the company that you are really interested in approaching? You could miss out on potentially important information.

Showing interest makes people feel valued, which is bound to go in your favour. When was the last time you were swayed by someone who showed no interest in what is important to you? The less connection there is between people, the easier it is for the other person to ignore your influence.

The important distinction is that you don't just *show* interest, but that you actually *are* interested. Turn on your curiosity. Wonder what makes people tick. Suspend judgement. Give them the benefit of the doubt.

How:

- Firstly, pay attention to what you think you already know about the person. What assumptions have you made? Separate facts from your opinion. Look for where you have attached your interpretation. You may be wrong. There may be other ways of viewing their actions or words. Begin by withholding judgement so that you can open your mind to being genuinely interested in them.

- Secondly, notice the other person's personal style. Are they sociable? Reserved? Thoughtful? Impulsive? If you have never learnt about different models of personality, it may be worth exploring a little. There are many theories and models that can help you understand why people are different. When it comes to personality traits, there is no right or wrong - but different types respond to different approaches.

- Learn to adapt your approach to suit the other person's personal style. Unfortunately, when we feel we aren't being understood or liked, out knee jerk reaction tends to be 'more' or ourselves - coming on stronger with the same approach. Think of the person abroad raising his voice to someone who doesn't speak his language. It's not going to help, is it? Try to work out what makes them tick, what is important to them, what they enjoy. Keep going until you can see the world through their eyes. Put yourself in their shoes. What does it feel like to be them? Learn to deliver your message taking what's in it for them into account.

- Look for clues and signs for topics to the person's interests and concerns. You can use them to build rapport and break the ice. *'Is that Japan? Did you enjoy it?' 'You look worried. Is the project behind schedule?'* Notice when you get a good response that indicates receptive ground.

- Create a bank of questions or lines of conversations you are comfortable to use. It depends to some degree on your confidence and style. If you are never stuck for words, that's great, but if nerves sometimes get the better of you, or you flounder, it can help enormously to have some ideas up your sleeve. It can also help you be more focused, even if you are a confident conversationalist.

- Look for the feelings behind the facts and the facts behind the feelings. By exploring these, you'll learn much about how the other person operates, which is useful for influencing. It means you can adapt your message to use language they will understand.

- Dig and delve (subtly!) then sift. What can you do for them? What can they do for you? How are you similar? How are you different?

How to get it wrong

Here's a story that we tell in The Job Interview Toolkit:

Amy rested on her laurels

Amy was approached by Ed, who she knew socially. He owned a local company and he had a vacancy that was ideal for her. Ed asked Amy to pop in for a chat about the job. She knew they got on well together and she had the right skill set. The vacancy hadn't even been advertised. What could go wrong? It was in the bag, surely?

She didn't get the job. Ed was cold called by a job seeker who impressed him deeply with her knowledge of his company and her research about his business sector.

She had done her homework well, analysed his needs and put together a compelling case on why she should be hired. Amy, on the other hand, took a casual approach and assumed their friendship was sufficient. She knows better now.

Summing up

Be interested in what makes the person you want to influence tick, find out what is going on with them and adapt your approach to suit their style.

Step Two

★ Be inescapable

No, this does not mean you need to be a stalker! It is about being a gentle reminder or consistent presence. You will be at the forefront of someone's consciousness, so they are less likely to forget you. Let's consider for a moment how we are influenced by others wanting to spread their message to us in this way.

Marketeers know that we need to be exposed to an advert many times before we buy the product or service. It takes a considerable time for us to move from *'I don't know it exists'* to *'I want it!'*. It's a gradual building up of exposure that eventually seeps into our consciousness. They call it "Effective frequency". Research has shown that on average, we need to see an advert about 20 times before we consider buying the product.

Think about it. At any one time, we have so many things competing for our attention, it is actually impossible for our brain to take on board everything we see and hear, so we only process information that we think is relevant or useful. Even then, our brain will delete it if we don't use it soon. The same goes for our messages. If our audience doesn't find us relevant, useful or appealing in some way, they will soon forget us. Even if they are interested at the time, it is all too easy for us to slip from their mind as other priorities compete.

Are you wondering if we can really transfer advertising theory to getting our own point across? How do we make sure people remember us for the right reasons, and hear what we have to say? How do we stop them forgetting us the minute we leave the room?

Here's an example

Think back to the last time you went to a busy bar. Can you tell me who was in it? If we had spoken right after you left, you could probably give me a pretty good run down on who was there. You might even know a couple of names. If I ask you the same question in a year's time, I doubt you would be able to tell me much – unless you knew the folk there already, or you'd run into them since and got to know them.

The same goes for all walks of life. We may meet someone we like, have a great conversation, but unless we bump into them again, we are unlikely, sadly, to store them in our memory. Have you been to regular networking events? They start being a sea of faces. If you go again, you will be relieved to see a familiar face or two. Third time you will smile at a few more people because you recognise them. Before you know it, you will be able to make a beeline for the people you know you want to spend time with.

If you want to be noticed, you will need to be focused on making and developing the connections that matter.

They're not interested in me...

Of course they're not. You told your boss last month that you'd be interested in moving into account management, you mentioned it to HR too. Nothing has happened, so obviously they don't think you're good enough. Maybe they think you're inexperienced, or just wouldn't get on with that team. You always thought that the team leader in that department didn't rate you highly. Perhaps you should look for another job, or perhaps you just resign yourself to staying where you are and just be thankful you have a job...

STOP RIGHT THERE!

Do you recognise these kind of thought patterns? You don't have any hard evidence about what's going on, so you assume the worst and let your mind fill the gaps. Your brain is made to try and make sense of things, so if you let it get carried away it will invent stories. Note these are stories, not facts. For each pseudo 'fact' it will attach the appropriate emotion, and then build in another, ahem, 'fact' into the sorry tale. Where does this get you? Go back to the "They're not interested in me" paragraph above. What unsubstantiated conclusions have been reached?

- I'm not good enough

- They are not on my side

- There is no hope for me here

- She doesn't like me

- My career is going nowhere   ...and so on.

When we tell ourselves messages like these, what emotions do we attach to our thoughts? Taking the list above, you might feel:

- Insecure

- Depressed

- Frustrated

- In despair

- Unmotivated

So tell, me how are you ever going to make a good impression in front of the right people if those are the emotions leaking out of your pores? The short answer is – you're not.

Not only will you not make a good impression when you have the opportunity, chances are that you will avoid potential lucky breaks because you don't have the confidence to see them through. You can't be inescapable if you are hiding in the broom cupboard, can you?

You know what to do

Break the negativity cycle. Replace negative thoughts with nourishing, uplifting positive ones. Take action to find out the truth in a situation before you start embroidering nasty, soul destroying lies into your head.

What do you think the truth is in the story above? Your career move may be top of your priority list, but it probably isn't your boss's. She will have many staff to manage, deadlines to meet, plans to make, senior management to negotiate with. If you want her to see how serious you are, its going to take more than mentioning it once to even enter her radar.

One more quick lesson from our friends in advertising - We all hit the 'unsubscribe' button regularly, don't we? The sender works on the basis that if we haven't unsubscribed, it is okay to keep contacting us, because we are still happy to receive communication from them.

Use the same principle. If you haven't been asked to stop calling someone, assume they don't mind hearing from you or seeing you. If this is a step too far for you and you think maybe they do mind, try asking. *"Can I give you a quick call next week?" "Is it ok if I stop by your office on Friday to show you my ideas?"*

Do you still need convincing?

Exposure

A piece of research by Harvey Coleman examined why people get promoted in many large organisations. He identified three factors:

- Being good at your job
- Having the right image
- Exposure (building contacts and raising your profile)

Which do you think was the most influential?

It found that exposure outstripped the other factors by miles at 60%. Having the right image was second at 30%, with job competence limping in last at 10%. Do you ever wonder how some mediocre performers get their jobs? Now you know. They look the part and mix in the right circles. You can be the best image consultant/dog groomer/ plumber in the world, but people will forget you – or won't even find you in the first place- unless they have reason to remember you.

Social media has a role to play here too. It's a huge topic in its own right, but you can use it to reinforce the message you want to send with human contact. Take the example we used earlier of wanting to join a project team. You could use LinkedIn to find relevant contacts, then make sure you share useful articles on project management that will appear in the newsfeed of the people you want to get in front of.

There are many ways you can use social media to forward your mission. If you're not very experienced it is worth spending time with someone who can help you with a strategy. It is better to do do one or two things well than many things badly – and remember, it is not a substitute for real interaction, so don't hide behind it.

Consistency

One last point before we look at how to be inescapable. We've been encouraging you to find your target and aim for it. This is all well and good, but pause for a moment and think of all the other people you run into who are not your top priority to hear the message you want to convey. I used to work with someone whose behaviour changed around senior management. She became in instant ball of smiley sunshine any time a senior manager visited, bending over backwards to help them in any way she could.

Unfortunately, she wasn't this accommodating, or pleasant to her everyday team mates. What message was she sending out? It certainly wasn't *"I value my colleagues"* or *"I'm always helpful"* Remember we talked about congruence? Everything we do needs to tell the same story if we are to be believed. If we are not believed, our integrity is questioned – and if we are not trusted, the power of our ability to influence is zilch.

Be consistently the person you want to be, not a part time version. This means being aware of the impact of your behaviour on everyone you come into contact with, not just that one special person. If you aim to be the person you want to be all the time, it will be much easier when it is really important to make the right impression.

I'm sure your thinking that it's a fine line between being a pain in the neck and being invisible – and it is. More often than not, we lean towards invisible because we don't want to be a nuisance – when in reality, we are not being a nuisance at all. Let's look at way of getting the balance right.

How

- Look for existing opportunities to be around the people you want to be in front of. This will be easier once you've mastered being interested, as you will pick up clues.

- Make new opportunities where you can. You can be by the coffee machine at the right time, take lunch in the right cafe, ask for a meeting, request an invitation to a meeting, suggest you both attend a conference you've found out about... have a brainstorm, get as many ideas as you can.

- Notice who has this person's ear. Work on getting close to them, too.

- Make it easy for your target. Remind them who you, and what you are interested in. Remember it's a two way street, though. Put some thought into thinking what you can do to make their day a little brighter too.

- Use the other person's preferred method of communication, and mirror their style. For example, you can match their level of formality, or alter your pace of speech.

- Remember that they have their own agenda. Acknowledging what is important to them will make them more inclined to listen to what matters to you.

- Use social media to strengthen your message. If your target suddenly decides to check you out on line, what will they find? Is it congruent with your message?

- Eliminate 'them and us' thinking. All you are doing is putting a psychological wall between you, making it harder to reach them.

An inescapable story

A long while ago, I was visiting a small, popular software company. The MD's phone rang just as we were about to begin our meeting, I gestured that it was fine to take the call.

*He had a brief conversation during which he laughed, and smiled a lot. When he came off the phone, he told me the caller had been a young lady who really wanted to work at the company. She rang **every week** to see if he had any vacancies. She was always good humoured and upbeat, and he was impressed with her attitude and tenacity.*

The MD told me that he didn't currently have any vacancies - but that when he did, he was going to hire her.

Summing up

Make it impossible for your target not to know you exist, in a positive way. Take or make opportunities to be in the right circle, at the right time and in the right place.

Step Three

 Be incisive

So far we've been interested in our target, so we are building up knowledge about what makes them the unique person they are, and we've thought about how we can make sure they know we exist and don't forget us. So far so good, but unless you want to become their golf partner or drinking buddy, you will need to make sure you don't forget to focus on what it is you want to achieve. This chapter will help you make sure.

Stuck for words?

Have you ever had the experience of struggling for words, yet over time you learnt to say much the same thing without any worry? I once worked for an organisation that was able to offer a free service. The funding dried up and we had to start charging clients. Many of my colleagues found it almost impossible to deal with this, but of course they had to.

A few weeks later, it had become second nature. The fears had been addressed, the words found and confidence had grown. Of course they could tell the clients about our fees – after all, the service was worth it.

Say it out loud

At the beginning of this book you were asked to clarify what it was you want to say and write it down, so you should have your message in language that is meaningful to you. Tell me, have you tried speaking it out loud?

Sometimes it is easy to say what is on our mind but unfortunately it isn't always. Often the more important the message is to us, the more likely we are to fluff our lines or chicken out completely. We find all kinds of excuses for failing to say what we really want; we ask ourselves a million times if the time is right, begin to waffle and our resolve evaporates.

Don't let the first time you have a great opportunity be the first time you say your message out loud. Make it as easy to speak out as *"White, one sugar please"*. Start by reading it aloud a few times to get familiar with the words. You will notice that the way we choose words when we write isn't the same as when we speak. You will need to be able to make your point in language you are comfortable using – and also in words that your target audience is able to understand and accept easily.

Play around with the words as you speak them. Think of different audiences, different circumstances, different emotions. Experiment with all of these.

Try changing your tone, pace, language. Try saying it with a smile, or gravely serious. Not only are you embedding the ability to speak it out in your brain, you are also giving yourself a repertoire of alternative approaches which will help you flex to any situation you might encounter.

Be an exocet missile!

I don't have first hand experience, but I understand that exocet missiles have a radar that follows their target, so they never miss. You could easily miss out on opportunities if you don't have your message primed and ready to fire. You'll need to get to the point, keep it relevant to your listener, have strategies for keeping on track, and be prepared to deal effectively with whatever response comes your way.

Think what is in it for them

You will also need to know why your target should spend any time listening to you. Frame your message so that not only is it language that appeals to them , but also makes it clear how they will benefit from taking your message on board.

A young Youth Worker was once allocated to a school, and she told me angrily that the Head Teacher showed no interest in her work, and obviously had not been properly briefed about why she was there. What do you make of that? At the time – and no doubt it is still the case – schools were being judged almost solely on academic league tables and were under huge pressure to achieve good results or risk losing their funding. I doubt that the head Teacher had any spare reserves to deal with other demands on his attention.

If it had been me, I would have made sure that I knew how good youth work can motivate students to achieve and so have a positive impact on exam results. I would mention it in my first few encounters with the Head Teacher. *"Here's how my work will help you do better in the league tables..."* Would that have got his attention?

You can grab someone's interest by introducing a new topic – more of that in Step Four - but it's usually good practice to link your message to the other persons interests, (If you don't know what these are, have another go at Step One) framed in the language they understand.

If you are struggling to get to grips with the concept of what's in it for them (which you might see referred to as 'WIIFMs - 'What's in it for me?'), here are some ideas:

What's in it for them?

It might be:

- A solution to a problem they are facing

- The chance to be seen as a good or caring person/colleague/boss

- Improved reputation or PR

- A more motivated worker

- A better profit margin

- A more harmonious team

- Contribution to society/charity/the greater good

- Less conflict in the home

- The opportunity to have better equipped staff

- One in the 'favour bank'

....etc

Do you see how this works? Go to where you message is written down, and add the WIIFM for your target.

How

- How can you steer the conversation? What topics/links will get you from your opening line to being able to deliver your message?

- Beware 'red flag' words. This means words that may make emotions flare, causing temporary 'blindness' to reason! If you make your target see red, you'll do worse than lose them instantly, you will lose any goodwill you have established. Think carefully before using any negative or emotive language that might cause an extreme response.

- Learn to blow your own trumpet without seeming arrogant. You may well be the only person that knows your passion, skills and motives, so be able to talk about yourself in a pragmatic, matter–of–fact way without sounding boastful of overly modest. This is as much about tone and style of delivery than it is about the language you choose. This in another thing you can practise aloud.

If this is a step too far for you, make sure the important information about you is documented somewhere you can refer to, or signpost to, for example a blog or LinkedIn profile

- Don't be afraid of pauses. Sometimes you need to let your words sink in. Don't rush to fill the silences.

- Be clear and concise. Using more words won't necessarily increase understanding. Check as you go *"Does that make sense to you?" "Have I explained that clearly?"*

- Think through their possible reactions. Run the scenario though in your mind. What will you do if they seem dismissive? Or ask you questions? Or respond with a bear hug?

- Be brave. You want them to hear this, so tell them. You will be glad you did.

Summing up

Get to the point, don't beat around the bush. Know your message, be well prepared and rehearsed. Be as laser sharp as an exocet missile. Focus, aim, fire!

* * *

Step Four

 ## ★ Be inspirational

So far, we've been interested in the other person, manoeuvred ourselves into their line of vision, and delivered our message. So far so good - but we still might be forgettable. Let's turn our mind to how we can go the extra mile to make them notice. Let's be inspirational! How can we 'wow' them? Yes, this is the tallest order so far, but by far the one that will get you the greatest results.

What does it mean?

This is a little tricky, as we are all inspired by different things.

Let's turn to the dictionary first.

> *"the process of being mentally stimulated to do or feel something, especially to do something creative."*

Often it might be that we are stirred by art, music, nature or beauty, but here we are focusing here on inspiration from people.

Consider times when other people have inspired you. Can you think of examples? What is it that someone else has done that has given you the wind beneath your wings to take on a new challenge, fight back, or take risks?

Was it:

- Their passion or enthusiasm?

- Their words of encouragement, telling you that you could do it?

- Their ability to see the situation from a different angle, giving you a new outlook?

- The way they helped you put things in perspective and see what is truly important?

- Their attitude to risk, telling you to seize the day, life is for living?

- Their reassurance, helping you cope with problems?

- Their positive attitude?

- The great example they set in all that they do?

- Their depth of knowledge, freely shared with you?

- Their ability to understand the heart of the matter?

- The way they challenged your thinking or actions?

- Their foresight?

- Their intuition?

- The calm and collected way they conduct themselves in the face of difficulties or pressure?

- The way they carry themselves with dignity, no matter how hard life gets?

- The amazing things they have achieved?

- Their generosity?

- Their energy, drive or determination?

- Something else? If so, what?

Over to you

You've guessed what is coming next. Now you are in the zone of thinking about what inspiration might be, it is time to look at the list and think about how you might inspire others. Self awareness is key here. It's no use saying how you can or can't be inspirational if your self perception is skewed. Take a cold hard look at the list above, or one you have produced yourself if you want to use your own words.

Which ones resonate with you? Which ones, modesty aside, do you think may apply to you? Which would you like to grow and develop? If you have confidantes you can trust, you could ask their opinion.

You cannot fabricate being inspirational, but you might be holding back in some areas. Are there positive aspects of your personality you could let stand out more? Are there times when you could be a ray of sunshine where there is usually gloom? We all fall into habits of behaviour without considering if we are acting in the best way to get us the results we want.

How Not To...

There is a worker in my local post sorting office whose job it is to deal with customers coming to pick up letters and parcels that have not been delivered, where the postman has left a card saying *"You were out...please collect this item from the sorting office"*. I guess she has to deal with a fair number of angry people from her body language. When she comes to the counter, she braces herself, squares her shoulders and wears a pretty serious *"Don't mess with me"* expression. Bearing in mind that behaviour breeds behaviour, she is pretty much asking customers to give her a hard time. She could disarm a high proportion of disgruntled customers by looking as if she was pleased to see them.

Sometimes aspects of our behaviour need reigning in rather than being allowed to roam free. It's possible to be so enthusiastic and excitable or grumpy and demanding that you become tiresome, and your words become lost as your audience writes you off as someone they cannot respect.

It's also possible to be too 'nice' to be inspirational. If you try too hard to never say no or please everybody, you may be seen as a pushover, too soft, or not knowing your own boundaries.

How

- Be inspired yourself – and let it show

- People feed off enthusiasm so nourish them. Share positive energy.

- If you feel down, be careful where you share it. We all need places we can offload with people we trust, but consider the impact on your reputation

- Set yourself high standards, model who you want to be

- Encourage others. Give positive feedback. If they mess up, help them move forward.

- Listen to yourself. Could you speak more clearly? Lower pitch? Be less monotone? Do you sound like someone you would want to listen to?

- Generosity can be inspiring. Give your time, expertise and support where you can.

Summing up

To be inspirational, know your passions, spread good vibes and contain your difficulties and emotional lows to a safe environment. Be prepared to step up generosity of spirit and know your own boundaries.

Step Five

★ Be increasing

I was working recently in a large food manufacturing company, and chatted over lunch to one of the senior managers. He told me about Joe, one of his staff. Joe was just one of the factory hands, which is a lowly position. Joe was aware that one aspect of the production process was very costly to the company. In his own time at home, he researched the issue online extensively, put his brain into gear, researched some more and then went to his boss with a suggestion.

Drum roll please...That suggestion saved the company three million pound per year. It wasn't in Joe's job description to find answers. He never would have found the solution based on his existing knowledge. He chose to invest his own time, and perhaps satisfy his own curiosity, to help his company. Even if he hadn't come up with a result, he would have known far more about how the business operated. I find his dedication and attitude totally inspiring.

Passive or active?

When it comes to finding explanations, improvements and solutions, are you passive or active? Here's the thing: Steps One to Four may be enough to get you to be able to deliver that message, but if your scenario is ongoing, say for example related to your career, it could get jaded over time. Same old you, same old message...

The limp lettuce test

Always have something new and fresh to bring to the table. Do you want to be the juicy, appetizing morsel that makes people gravitate towards you, or are you happy being the limp, stale old offering that people usually pass by? Standing still is not an option when the word is moving swiftly around us. In real terms, it is the equivalent of going backwards.

If you've read Stephen Covey's 'Seven Habits of Highly Effective People', you'll recognise that what we are talking about here is what Covey calls sharpening the saw – the practice of making sure we are continually growing, learning and developing.

Surviving or thriving?

I know that we are learning all the time, trying to keep up with technology and changes in the marketplace. Many of us have CPD (continuous professional development) thrust upon us, to keep us up to date with our industry and legislation around it. This is reacting to the world we live in, a necessary survival skill.

If you have a message to deliver, ambitions, want a better way of living, we need more than survival – we need to thrive. This means taking ownership of our learning; choosing what will be beneficial to us, and help us reach our dreams rather than just taking what comes our way. Take control of your development so that you can grow into the person you want be, not the person someone else thinks you should be.

I can hear you screaming *'But I don't have time to do any more learning!'* As your mother rightly said, where there is a will, there is a way. You are unique. I doubt you learn in exactly the same way as me. You need to try a few things to find out what works best for you – but be honest with yourself. It won't work if you tell yourself you will read all day if you have a short attention span (like me!). All that will happen is that you will feel a failure, which will demotivate you. It's a downward spiral.

There are many resources on how to learn. You might like to find a learning styles questionnaire on line if you have never done one, to help you work out which might suit you. There's not space to list them all here, instead here are a few tips for fitting learning into a busy lifestyle.

How

- Make a note of things you'd like to know about. You could jot them on your To Do list, in your diary or an online notebook, or an app on your phone. When you have some time, do some research.

- Download podcasts – there are some really great ones out there that will keep you up to date. I listen to them when I'm gardening, driving, ironing or in the bath.

- Audio books – similar to podcasts, but if you need meatier information, or want a specific book, you don't have to actually find time to read it.

- Read blogs. Many successful professionals share insights on a regular basis. Be highly selective or you could drown.

- Use You Tube. If you think You Tube is just for questionable pop videos and talking dogs, think again!

- Watch or listen to Ted talks. I often will put one on late at night and listen before I sleep.

- Be accountable. If you never seem to get round to it, start or join a group (there are some business book clubs around, for example), or make a pact with a colleague or friend. Just telling someone you are going to do it is often enough to make that move.

- Networking meetings often have guest speakers that share useful information. Keep an eye on the topics coming up in your area.

- Then there are all the well established ways of learning you probably know about. Join a course, try distance learning such as The Open University, do an online course (www.alison.com has loads for free).

There isn't really an excuse not to, is there?

Summing up

Not learning is not an option. It is stagnation. Find ways to keep growing your skills, knowledge and behaviour so that other people's respect for you grows with every conversation.

Putting the Pieces Together

There you have it!

What will you do now?

Now it is time to work out where you go from here. We started with some searching questions to help you be clear about your message - the importance of understanding what is important to say, who to, and why. That alone may have given you several action points.

Before we move on to planning for action, let's recap on the five steps. Here is a summary:

1. Be Interested

Be interested in what makes the person you want to influence tick, adapt to their style, and find out what is going on with them.

2. Be Inescapable

Make it impossible for your target not to know you exist, in a positive way. Take or make opportunities to be in the right circle, at the right time and in the right place.

3. Be Incisive

Get to the point, don't beat around the bush. Know your message, be well prepared and rehearsed. Be as laser sharp as an exocet missile. Focus, aim, fire!

4. Be Inspirational

To be inspirational, know your passions, spread good vibes and contain your difficulties and emotional lows to a safe environment. Be prepared to step up generosity of spirit and know your own boundaries.

5. Be Increasing

Not learning is not an option. It is stagnation. Find ways to keep growing your skills, knowledge and behaviour so that your targets respect for you grows with every conversation.

Putting it all together

You may have been expecting a book just about communication skills, or assertiveness. Reading the summary above, no doubt you realise that to be an effective influencer of others takes more than being a good speaker - you need to take command of what goes on the inside of you as well as the outside.

It also is not all about you. Of course your agenda, goals and dreams are important to you - as are everyone else's to them. Being prepared to see the world through the eyes of others, and to help them achieve their goals will increase your perspective; you will find opportunities to grow and synergies between you.

The respect others have for you will grow too, increasing your field of influence.

Plan some actions

Working through the five steps may also have generated thoughts about areas for development. Hopefully there will be a handful of actions you can start on straight away too, and you are raring to go.

Whoa! Hold that horse!

Don't overwhelm yourself. I mentioned the importance of prioritising action points earlier. If you have more than half a dozen things to do on your list, you are in danger of losing focus and achieving none of them. Let's make sure you are clear about what your actions are, and also how you are going to make sure they happen.

Firstly, write down everything you want to achieve that has come to mind. Have a look through the five steps to make sure that you have them covered. At this stage, don't worry if your action points are vague or woolly. Just get everything down, and work at refining them later.

Make an Action Plan

Here are some tips to help you turn your thought into a strong plan of action:

- Group similar points together. You might be able to come up with two or three themes.

- Is there a hierarchy, ie one thing you need to do before you can do another? Or things that can not happen until something else is in place?

- Sometimes it's easier to work with pen and paper than on a screen, away from distractions. You could use a mind map to help you.

- Listen to your gut feeling. What do you really want to do first? What would you rather avoid? Try and understand what it is telling you. Our intuition is our brain's store of what it has learnt from past experience - often we know more than we give ourselves credit for. It may be that deep down inside you know what is most important. Or it may be that you are telling yourself untruths, based on fear and anxieties.

- Set your priorities. Be realistic about what is achievable. Park everything else on the list until you have made progress with your top priorities.

- Make each action point SMART. (Specific, measurable, achievable, realistic, time bound).

- Break down each action point into small steps. This way you can see your progress more easily.

A good action plan will contain the aims, details about the steps you will take, the date you will have it done by, and a place where you can record progress. Devise a format that works for you. You could find an example on line, but personalise it so that it inspires and motivates you - Colours, fonts, even pictures might help.

Making sure you get there

New behaviour can take up to six months to embed, before it becomes a natural part of the new you. Old habits can take even longer to lose. Be kind to yourself on the journey. If you find yourself struggling, think about finding a coach to help you. This is exactly the kind of job they love! Here a few other things that will help:

Reflection

Reflection is an important part of the learning cycle. When you have taken a step, think about how well you did. If you could have done anything differently, work out how. If it was not successful, work out why.

Amend your action plan if you have been too ambitious. When you have taken the learning from the event, move on. Do not allow yourself to worry or beat yourself up.

Put review dates in your diary. Analyse what you have achieved. If there are things you have not progressed as far as you would have liked, there are two things to do. Firstly, revisit the action point. Is it still relevant? Have the goalposts moved? Does it need refining to make it workable? If it is still on the list, take another look at what is holding you back. Are there underlying factors that need addressing?

Your Action Plan is not cast in stone, it is a living, organic document. Be prepared to refine and amend it as your progress unfurls.

Accountability

It's easy to let things slide if we only have ourselves to answer to. Who else could hold you responsible? It could be your manager, a colleague, coach, mentor or friend. If you are not confident in your self motivation, or you begin to wane, find someone you trust to share your action plan with. Maybe you can do the same for them.

Lastly... Rewards

Changing behaviour takes persistence and determination. You deserve to reward yourself for any step forward, not matter how small. How will you reward yourself? Make a list of treats - books, music, food, drink, activities, time with friends.... Whatever works for you. You've earned it!

Index

About the Author

Julie Cooper

Hello. I'm a trainer, coach and author specialising in one to one skills. I understand that busy people want accessible, practical information. They rarely have time or inclination to read complicated tomes, which is why my books are packed with instantly usable techniques and tips. I also coach other professionals to help them turn their ideas into a book.

Please do check out my company, Spring Development (www.springdevelopment.net) which offers training and development to organisations and individuals that want to flourish and get the best out of their working lives. You can find my books at www.springpublishing.net.

I recently moved to Banbury in Oxfordshire, UK after many years in The Fens, working in and around Cambridgeshire. Outside of work, I enjoy looking after my newly inherited amazingly beautiful garden, exploring The Cotswolds, and seeking out live music, arts and crafts.

Other books By Julie Cooper:

Face to Face in the Workplace: A handbook of Strategies for Effective Discussions ISBN 978-0955968037

Looking to improve your management skills? This is an accessible guide to every meeting, discussion or difficult conversation you will need to have.

Written for busy people who need quick solutions, Face to Face in the Workplace will equip you with all the tools and strategies you'll need to get it right every time.

Step by step frameworks will guide you in getting the best out of the people you manage, and yourself. You will: have more productive discussions that please everyone involved; save time by knowing how to prepare effectively; never have to worry about what to say in difficult meetings; learn to get your point over more effectively; improve your people management skills - and your career prospects.

Included: Assertive behaviour, Explaining, Listening, Interviewing applicants ,Making someone redundant , Saying no, Shutting people up, Introducing change, Self awareness, Dismissing a member of staff, Personality styles, Challenging , Questioning, Credibility, Rapport, Body language, Respect , Appraisals, Return to work interviews, Challenging attitude, Coaching, Feedback, Conflict, The Dark Triad, Negotiating , Delegating, Exit interviews, Instructing, Influencing, Inappropriate Behaviour, Managing your Boss, Mentoring, Performance gaps, Praising, Supervising, Reprimanding, Supporting through change, 360° feedback.

"This year's Must Have book" **HR Director magazine**

Co-Authored with Ann Reynolds:

The One to One Toolkit: Tips and Strategies for Advisers, Coaches and Mentors

by Julie Cooper and Ann Reynolds   ISBN 978-0955968051

Does your job involves helping people to move forward in their career, learning, or personal development? If so, this book is for you. It aims to meet the needs of people employed in the field of advice and guidance in a practical, user friendly way.

It explains useful models, suggests strategies for dealing with difficulties, and provides powerful, memorable tools to use with clients.

Part One takes you, step by step, through a tried and trusted model for giving advice, including highlighting dangers and difficulties in a "how to" manner.

Part Two provides a more in depth model, focusing on guidance, explaining how to help your client in a professional manner when their needs are more complex.

Part Three is The Toolkit - a collection of bite sized theories, tips, exercises and strategies that can be used with clients in a one to one setting. Topics include decision making, changing perception, expanding horizons, positive thinking, learning and coaching.. Widely used as a text for organisations training advisers.

"I love this little book. It gives me new guidance ideas every time I open it." **Amazon review**

• • •

The Groupwork Toolkit: How To Convert Your One To One Advice Skills To Work With Groups

by Ann Reynolds and Julie Cooper ISBN 978-0955968013

The Groupwork Toolkit makes group work easy for anyone used to working one to one, by showing you how to recognise and transfer the skills you already have.

Advisers, coaches and mentors have a wealth of interpersonal and communication skills, but may lack the experience and confidence to transfer them successfully to running groups. The Groupwork Toolkit can help.

It demystifies group work, and gives you the confidence and knowledge you need to facilitate groups, whether your group are learning new skills, or have come for advice or guidance. It explains how you can deliver brilliant groupwork by planning well, setting objectives and using a variety of training techniques.

How people learn is covered, explaining the different ways people learn so you can adapt your style and methods to meet the needs of each group. There is a step by step model for producing a session plan, with plenty of practical tips and activities to use. Sample session plans are also included.

Lastly, sound advice on how to manage a group includes keeping the group involved and interested, and how to handle those difficult situations and individuals. If you need to provide group guidance, deliver career or job search sessions, this is the book for you.

"The Group Work Tool Kit saved my life when I was doing my group work assessment for the QCG". Francesca Hall

The Job Interview Toolkit: Exercises to get you fit for your interview

by Ann Reynolds and Julie Cooper   ISBN 978-0955968020

The Job Interview Toolkit is practical, easy to follow guide to preparing for interviews, ideal for job seekers of all ages, especially the young and those returning to work after a break.

It contains a selection of activities, organised in the five-step TAPAS programme, designed to get you fit to perform like a star on the day. Its easy to read format make it accessible to job seekers of all ages. Advisers will find ideas for working with their clients too.

This book is:

Easy to read – short sections, illustrations and diagrams, examples and danger stories

Practical – with things to do, questions to answer, photos to comment on, things to practise with a friend. Most of us learn best by doing, so you will find a five-step programme of exercises to get you fit and ready for the interview (the really important facts are there too).

A simple framework that is easy to learn:T-A-P-A-S. Think – Analyse   –   Prepare   –   Adjust   –   Shine!

This book will make sure you know what to do, perform at your best and sell yourself brilliantly!

*"I re-read it before my last interview - and got the job! "***Micky Waycot**

Keep in touch!

I'd love to hear if you have any success stories using the strategies in this book. Please do send your stories to Julie@springpublishing.co.uk

Have you enjoyed this book?

If so, please do leave a review. You can either email it directly to us, and we can include it on the Spring Publishing website (www.springpublishing.co.uk). Alternatively, you can leave it Amazon, or anywhere else readers will find it.

Need a Workshop?

If your organisation would like a workshop, conference speaker or training event, Julie is available - please do get in touch. Our UK phone number is 0845 5197 571, or email jule@springdevelopment.net.

Julie's website is www.springdevelopment.net.

Notes